JACK
HORNER

LIVING WITH DINOSAURS

JACK HORNER

LIVING WITH DINOSAURS

BY DON LESSEM

ILLUSTRATED BY JANET HAMLIN

Scientific
American
BOOKS FOR YOUNG READERS

W. H. FREEMAN AND COMPANY ◆ NEW YORK

Book design by Debora Smith

Scientific American Books for Young Readers is an imprint of
W.H. Freeman and Company, 41 Madison Avenue
New York, New York 10010

Library of Congress Cataloging-in-Publication Data

Lessem, Don.

Jack Horner: living with dinosaurs / by Don Lessem;

illustrated by Janet Hamlin.

Includes biographical references and index.

ISBN 0-7167-6546-2 — ISBN 0-7167-6549-7 (pbk.)

Horner, John R.—Juvenile literature. 2. Paleontologists—United States—Biography—
Juvenile literature. [1. Horner, John R. 2. Paleontologists.] I. Hamlin, Janet, ill. II. Title.

QE707.H67L47 1994

567.9'1'092—dc20

[B]

94-17993

CIP

AC

Printed in the United States of America

10 9 8 7 6 5 4 3 2 1

To Drs. Peter Dodson,
David Weishampel, and Steven Gittelman—
my other dinosaur pals

CONTENTS

CHAPTER 1

Home, Home on the Range

Little Jack Horner sat in a corner. At least, that's how the nursery rhyme goes.

In real life, little Jack Horner walked around Montana with his head down and his eyes wide open. Little Jack Horner was looking for dinosaurs.

Jack Horner is grown now, and he finds dinosaurs all the time. He's been finding them since he was a kid in the 1950s. He's found eggs and babies and whole herds of dinosaurs, and he's learned more about how those wonderful animals lived than perhaps anyone else.

Jack Horner is now Dr. Horner, the world's most famous dinosaur scientist. He is the paleontologist—a scientist who studies ancient life—upon whom the book and movie *Jurassic Park* is modeled. Jack was an adviser to the movie. He travels the world giving talks, writing books, and looking for dinosaurs. His spectacular finds have changed the way all of us imagine dinosaurs.

Jack Horner did most of his discovering by walking around the state of Montana, sometimes even getting down on his hands and knees and crawling, to find fossils—traces of ancient life. And he's not done looking for, or finding, dinosaurs. This is his story.

You could call Jack Horner by his proper name, John R. Horner. That's how he is listed at the Museum of the Rockies in Bozeman,

Montana: "Dr. John R. Horner, Curator of Paleontology." "Dr." is an honorary title awarded to him by the University of Montana. Since he never finished college, being called "Dr." doesn't suit him. And as for the "John" part—well, that's the name his father goes by. Jack Horner has always liked being called just plain "Jack."

For as long as he can remember, he has liked nothing better than to be out on his own, collecting stuff. As Jack's dad recalls, "He was always fiddling with some fossils."

Montana is a spectacular state, full of beautiful lakes, pine woods, and snow-capped mountains. But the part of Montana where Jack grew up had none of those handsome features.

Jack's home was in Shelby, a railroad town in the dusty badlands of northwestern Montana, near the Canadian border. Flat and wind-swept, it's bitter cold most of the year. In summer it's blazing hot.

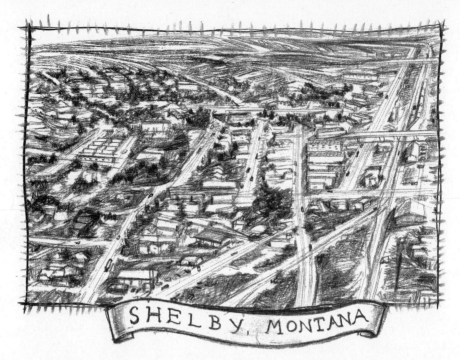

SHELBY, MONTANA

Jack Dempsey, a heavyweight boxing champion of the 1920s, came from Shelby and once fought for his title there. Aside from that fight, not a lot has gone on in Shelby that people elsewhere have heard about. Jack Horner grew up in Shelby because that's where his dad kept a gravel business.

Jack picked up lots of shale, gray rocks made from ancient mud—some with fossils in them—around the house where he grew up. The rocks were formed 75 million years ago, at the time when some of the last dinosaurs lived.

At that time, a shallow sea lay across what is now Shelby, Montana. The sea stretched all the way from what is now northern Canada to Mexico.

Dinosaurs lived on land, not in that sea or any other, so the first fossils Jack found were clams and fish, not dinosaurs.

But young Jack also spent time farther west in Montana, at his dad's ranch in the foothills of the Rocky Mountains. Seventy-five million years ago, the sea stopped short of the Rockies, so the rocks out there were dry land for dinosaurs then. Dinosaurs lived there—and died there. So those rocks had dinosaur fossils in them.

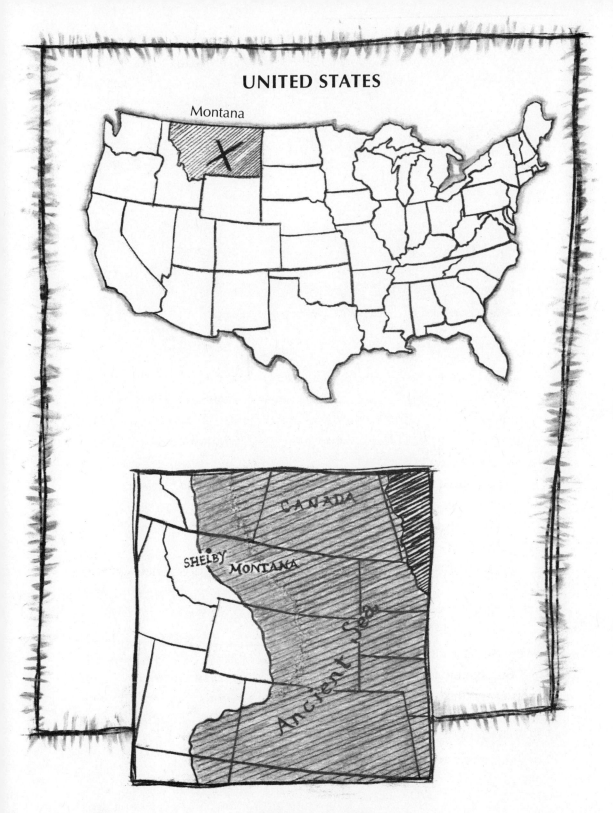

UNITED STATES

Montana

X

SHELBY MONTANA

CANADA

Ancient Seas

75 million years ago

Jack found his first dinosaur bone at the ranch when he was eight years old. It wasn't much of a fossil. Good dinosaur skeletons are hard to come by anyplace. But bits and pieces of dinosaur bone are scattered all over the hills and gullies just east of the Montana Rockies. Around the wide open country, dinosaur bones are easier to come across than people are. But to Jack that piece of fossil bone was special, because *he* found it. It's still special to him—he has it today.

From the moment he found that first fossil, Jack Horner was certain what he was going to do with his life. Lots of kids think they know what they are going to do when they grow up. Some want to be President. Others want to be ball players, or actors. For many reasons, though, most people end up as grown-ups working at something very different from what they imagined when they were eight.

But Jack Horner never changed his mind about what he was going to do. "I decided then I'd study dinosaurs. And not just any dinosaurs. Duckbilled dinosaurs." He was on his way to becoming a paleontologist.

Back home in Shelby, no one had ever found any dinosaurs, but that didn't stop Jack from looking. A gangly boy with a long stride, he scoured the countryside looking for fossils. "He'd walk ten miles an hour, his dad recalls. "Nobody could keep up with him."

Not that anyone tried to fossil-hunt with Jack. Not his dad, his mom, nor his little brother. "None of us cared a bit about fossils. We still don't," says his father.

Jack was a quiet boy. "Yup" and "nope" went a long way for him. Jack still doesn't talk much, except if you ask him about dinosaurs. Spending most of his time on his own, walking and collecting ancient clamshells and other sea fossils, suited Jack. When he wasn't out collecting, he was in the basement cleaning and studying what he'd found. And sometimes he did a little schoolwork, too.

The truth is, Jack didn't care much for any subjects in school. After all, they weren't teaching about dinosaurs. Besides, Jack had a hard time sorting out numbers and letters. The figures looked backward, unclear.

Jack had, and still has, a learning disability. The problem is called *dyslexia*. Today, schools test for dyslexia. When they find it, they give the student special learning exercises to help overcome the problem.

But when Jack went to school, not many people knew about dyslexia. Jack didn't. Neither did his teachers. They figured he didn't do well because he was a slow learner and not much interested in school. They were right only about his not being interested.

Jack kept trying, though, because he knew he couldn't be a paleontologist unless he finished college and took still more courses after that. Somehow, Jack graduated from high school. "I think the teachers were being generous," says his dad.

When Jack moved out of the house to go to college, his dad decided to clean out Jack's collection of rocks and fossils from the basement. "I took three truckloads to the dump to get rid of that stuff," Mr. Horner remembers. Jack wasn't upset. By then, he knew the landscape pretty well. He knew just where to go to find more fossils.

It was school that was a problem. Jack found the teachers weren't so generous at the University of Montana. He flunked out.

When he failed at the university in 1965, the Marines drafted him to fight in the Vietnam War. Jack wound up doing much more spying than fighting. He spent a year in the jungle, often alone, looking for enemy soldiers. He enjoyed walking around alone in the wilderness. After all, that was what he had done in Montana, although the landscape was very different. Still, Jack recalls, "I was glad when I was done in Vietnam. It was a hard, scary job."

When he finished his duty in the Marines, Jack tried college again. He took every geology and biology course offered at the University of Montana. To get a degree in paleontology, however, he also needed to take courses in math, English, and foreign languages. Those courses, especially the languages, were hard for Jack. He failed again. And again. In all, he flunked out seven times. His dream of becoming a dinosaur paleontologist seemed to be vanishing in the light of day.

CHAPTER 2

East Is East, But West Is Best

When Jack finally gave up on college in 1973, he worked for a while driving a gravel truck for his dad. Then he drove a big tractor-trailer, delivering fertilizer all over Montana. Jack often stopped that truck to go dinosaur hunting. "When I'd come to what seemed like a fossilly area," he has said, "I'd just stop, unhook my trailer, and drive off across the badlands in that tractor to look for dinosaur bones."

Jack needed to support himself, his young wife, and their son, Jason. But Jack figured he'd get himself a job at a college with a pale-ontology department. Those departments had fossil collections, and the fossils in those collections needed to be prepared.

You don't just dig up a dinosaur and put it on display. You take it out of the ground with plenty of dirt and rock still around it for protection. Then, back in the laboratory, a fossil worker, called a preparator, cleans the fossil.

Taking off the dirt is delicate, difficult work. Preparators use dentists' tools and toothbrushes and little motorized hammers to clean fossils. They squirt on dabs of special glues to mend broken fossil pieces.

Cleaning and preparing a single bone can take months. Fossil preparation is hard to learn, but Jack Horner already knew how to care for fossils. After all, he'd been collecting fossils nearly all his life.

Jack went to work cleaning fossils at the University of Montana. He worked at other jobs too, but he kept his eyes open for opportunities to learn more about dinosaurs. When a job for a fossil preparator opened up at Princeton University in New Jersey—one of the nation's leading research universities—Jack applied.

Jack was working on a combine, harvesting wheat, when word came he'd got the Princeton job. Jack didn't even know where Princeton was, and he told his new paleontologist boss, "I'll just drive east until I hit the ocean, and then I'll look around."

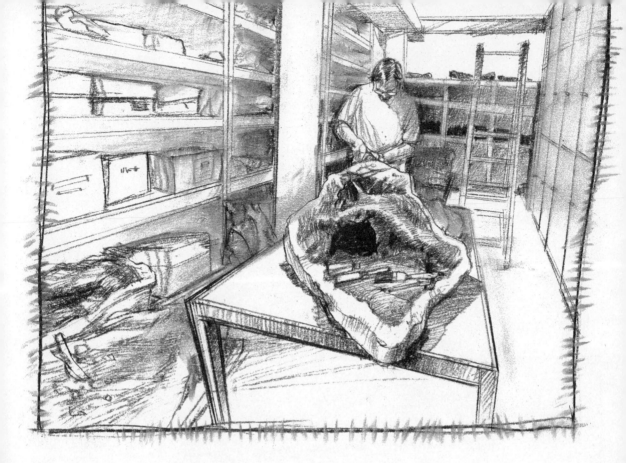

Preparator's room and storage

So Jack Horner went east. He didn't like it much. The people talked too fast, the streets were too crowded, the food was too fancy. The East was foreign to him, but Jack stayed seven years. He learned a lot about dinosaurs in that time, sitting in on classes, talking with the paleontology professors. Donald Baird, the Princeton paleontologist who was Jack's boss, remembers: "We thought we were getting a preparator, a guy who hadn't finished college. But this fellow knew more about the dinosaurs in our collection than any of us did."

In the basement of the museum, Jack found some dinosaur bones still in their plaster jackets, in which they had been shipped for protection. They'd been that way for more than seventy-five years, since Earl Douglass, a famous paleontologist, had collected them.

It was Horner's luck that these were the bones of duckbills and that they came from Montana. They were unusual because they came from young animals—"teenagers." Jack cleaned the bones, studied them, and wrote his first scientific paper about them. "It wasn't easy for him, being dyslexic, to write that paper, but he did a top-notch job," Dr. Baird remembers.

Princeton is an hour's drive from New York City, one of Jack Horner's least favorite places. But the American Museum of Natural History in New York holds the world's largest dinosaur collection, including lots of duckbilled dinosaurs. So every Saturday, Jack went to the museum to study its fossils.

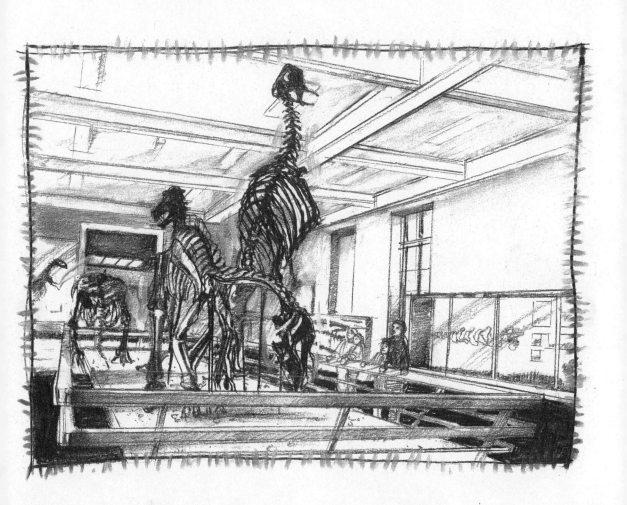

In the summer, paleontologists often do "field work"—dig in rocky, bare places at the far corners of the earth. Jack Horner joined Dr. Baird and a young Yale University paleontology student named Paul Olsen "in the field" in Nova Scotia. In the ocean-shore cliffs, Paul found tiny bones from a full-grown dinosaur no bigger than a turkey. These were the first scraps ever found in Canada of a dinosaur from the Jurassic Period—the middle period of dinosaur life. Jack helped piece these fossils together.

Jack had other field sites and fossils back in Montana in mind for himself. Each year he could hardly wait for school to end and summer vacation to begin. He'd pack his family into the car and head west, driving eighteen hours a day or more, until he was in Big Sky country again.

Back home, Jack would be out hiking, looking for dinosaur bones. He had a companion on many of these trips, Bob Makela. Bob and Jack had met in college and became best friends. Bob was now a high school science teacher, a friendly, gentle bear of a man, with a handy touch. And he was fearless. Bob used to cradle Gila monsters—poisonous reptiles—in his arms. In Bob's hands they were very well behaved.

With Bob, Jack had been studying the land of western Montana for years. They made their fossil hunts into great adventures, sometimes living only on what they could find and kill. As Jack recalls, "Squirrel tastes pretty good when you get used to it."

But Jack was looking for more than adventure and scattered fossils. After all, scientists had been finding dinosaurs in Montana for generations. Jack wanted to understand how those dinosaurs *lived*. What did they eat? How did they grow up? Did they live alone or in groups? Did they migrate or stay in one place? Did they prefer the mountains or the river deltas?

So many questions. And so few answers. When Jack Horner began asking those questions in the 1970s, we knew only a little more than half the kinds of dinosaurs we know about today. No one had ever found eggs or nests of dinosaurs in North America. No one had ever found a dinosaur embryo anywhere. Bones of young dinosaurs were almost unknown. The lives—and deaths—of dinosaurs, duckbills included, were great mysteries.

Jack didn't know the answers to any of these questions, either. In western Montana, the land he knew and loved, he hoped to find the evidence to begin answering some of them. Jack read up on how that land was formed, how the seaway had expanded and contracted over millions of years.

PALEOZOLC	DEVONIAN	CARBONIFEROUS	PERMIAN	TRIASSIC	JURASSIC	CRETACEOUS	CENOZOIC
600 million	420 million	350 million	300 million	235 million	208 million	144 million	65 million
years ago	years ago	years ago	years ago	years ago	years ago	years ago	years ago

THE AGE OF DINOSAURS

Charles Gilmore, a paleontologist from the early 1900s, had found many fossils in western Montana. In those days, paleontologists were mainly interested in collecting trophy skeletons to mount for display in their museums. How dinosaurs actually lived was not of as much interest to scientists from Dr. Gilmore's time as it is to Jack and to other scientists today. Maybe that's why Jack Horner and Don Baird made a startling discovery when they went to the Smithsonian Institution in Washington, D.C., and rummaged through Gilmore's collection.

Charles Gilmore had collected eggshells in Montana. They were the first dinosaur eggshell pieces found in North America. Gilmore, like other scientists of his time, thought so little of the eggshells' importance that he didn't even bother to write up his discovery.

But Jack Horner thought those eggshells were important. Like the young dinosaur bones Jack had studied at Princeton, these came from western Montana. Wherever that site was, there had to be more eggshells. In the summer of 1977 Jack found his first dinosaur egg. It was on his father's ranch, south of Gilmore's eggshell discoveries. Only Jack didn't know he'd found an egg. "I didn't know what it was till Dr. Baird said, 'It looks like an eggshell to me.'" The egg hunt had begun.

CHAPTER 3

Hot on the Trail

Jack and Bob Makela went back to Montana in the summer of 1978, beginning with the site where Earl Douglass had found juvenile dinosaur bones. Jack and Bob were looking for whole eggs, maybe even baby dinosaurs. When they arrived, it was raining. It kept raining for three days. Knee-deep in mud, they had no chance to finding fossils.

So Jack and Bob gave up and headed off south. When they came to the tiny town of Bynum, they decided to stop for a look around a local rock shop. The shop owners, John and Marion Brandvold, had also collected a lot of fossil bones. They asked Jack if he could identify some little bones they kept in their house.

"They weren't much to look at, just two dusty pieces of gray bone," Jack recalls in his book *Digging Dinosaurs*. But when Jack Horner saw the bones, he felt his heart race. These were the bones of duckbilled dinosaurs, which Jack knew grew to be thirty feet long. The long bones of duckbills, such as the thigh bone, measured five feet long and more than two feet wide. The bones the Brandvolds had found were shaped exactly like duckbilled dinosaur thigh bones. But these leg bones were smaller than Jack's thumb!

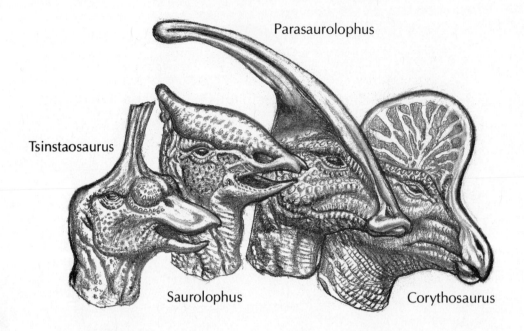

Parasaurolophus

Tsinstaosaurus

Saurolophus

Corythosaurus

The Brandvolds had filled up a coffee can with tiny duckbill bones. When Jack and Bob examined them all, they realized they had parts of at least four baby duckbills.

Instantly Jack knew he was on the trail of something few scientists had ever seen, a burial ground of young dinosaurs. Jack called Don Baird, his Princeton professor, and told him of the coffee can full of rare bones. Dr. Baird extended Jack's vacation and sent him five hundred dollars for digging expenses.

Jack and Bob headed for the source of the fossils—a bare patch of plains broken by small hills and gullies, near the sleepy town of Choteau, within sight of the Rockies.

There the Brandvolds led Jack and Bob to the Peebles family ranch. They led the men to one little hill littered with pebbles of many kinds and with slightly larger, gray-black bits. The dark pieces were the bones of baby dinosaurs.

Working quickly, Jack and Bob dug out a six-foot-wide chunk of green mudstone, the rock that contained the fossils. The piece they took out left a hole shaped like a big bowl surrounded by red mud.

That's when Jack and Bob realized the bones they were collecting came from a hole once dug as a nest by a duckbilled dinosaur. The hole had filled in with different-colored mud. For three days, Jack and Bob dug up nest-shaped clumps of green mud. They filled up burlap bags and brought them to Bob's backyard to prepare the fossils inside them.

At Bob's house they carefully sifted the dirt through screens until they had separated fossils of fifteen different baby dinosaurs. All of them belonged to dinosaurs less than three feet long!

Jack didn't know what had killed these baby dinosaurs. The bones hadn't been chewed by meat-eaters. But from these bones he could figure out a lot about how those dinosaurs lived.

The dinosaurs were not newborns. Their tiny teeth were already worn from chewing plants. Jack couldn't tell what kind of duckbill these babies belonged to, until the Brandvolds found a skull near one

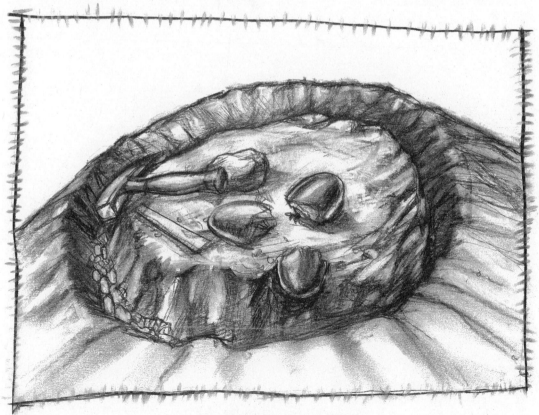

Maiasaura nest excavation

Maiasaura and young

nest. The skull came from a full-grown duckbill of an unfamiliar variety, with a long snout and no crest on its head. Perhaps this was the parent dinosaur that had cared for the babies in the nest.

So Don Baird thought up a name for this new dinosaur that cared for its young: *Maiasaura peeblesorum.* "Maia" means good mother. The second name honors the Peebles family, on whose ranch it was found.

Jack and Bob returned to the site during the following three summers, with crews of as many as ten volunteer helpers. Bob Makela created a camp complete with root cellar, kitchen, loading platform, and solar shower made from a tire tube. Bob even designed a waterslide-like chute for getting rocks down from the hill where the eggs and bones were found. Sometimes the crew would slide down after the rocks, and jokes about skiing down "Egg Mountain" gave the hill its name.

Jack and his team were scouting for more eggs and nests. It was painful work, done crawling on hands and knees over rocky ground. It was even dangerous. "It's the last place in America," Jack has said, "that still has the grizzly bear in its original habitat. Out on the plains. Do you know what it's like to be on your knees, looking for dinosaur bones—and at the same time looking over your shoulder for grizzly? It's *exciting.*"

Jack's team didn't run into any grizzlies. They did find many more nests, spaced as close as thirty feet from one another. That's about the length of an adult *Maiasaura.* Inside the nests they found oval eggs about eight inches long.

Jack realized that what he was digging up was a nesting colony of duckbills from 75 million years ago—like a seagull nesting colony today. Perhaps hundreds or thousands of these giant animals had nested side by side, hatching their eggs and rearing their young. Clam and snail fossils and mudstone rocks indicated to Jack that in dinosaur time Egg Mountain had not been a hill but a low, flat island.

Egg Mountain finds

Jack studied the ends of the nestlings' bones and saw they were still soft. That meant the babies were not able to walk soon after birth. For them to survive, a parent would have to care for them in the nest.

Fossils of babies of different sizes in the same nest showed that these babies grew fast. While still in the nest, they at least doubled in size. Just out of the egg they were fourteen inches long. In the same nest other babies were three and a half feet long.

As Jack pieced these fossils and their meaning together, he could tell an astonishing, true story never heard before in dinosaur science.

CHAPTER 4

The Riches of Egg Mountain

Imagine a huge plain a hundred miles from the sea. Among trampled bushes are mounds of mud: nests scooped out by huge duck-bills. All around, the adults are honking and bleating as they walk to the streamside to gather berries. Rotting vegetation covers some un-hatched eggs to keep them warm. Other nests are full of squawking, helpless babies with big eyes and wide-open mouths.

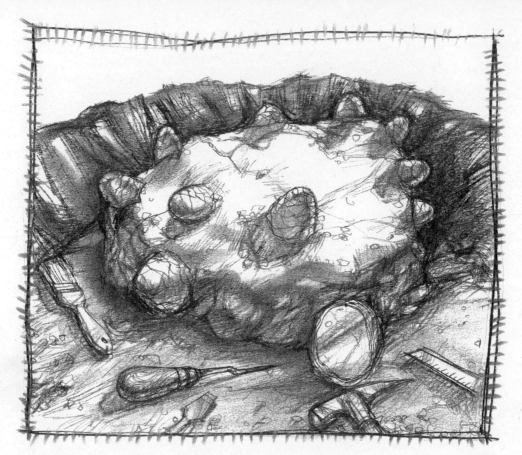

Egg Mountain eggs and nest

This is the story Jack's *Maiasaura* bones told. When the news of the "good mother" dinosaurs first appeared, many people, including other dinosaur scientists, were skeptical. Dinosaur paleontologist Dr. Peter Dodson of the University of Pennsylvania recalls, "I thought Jack had been out in the sun too long without his hat on." Dr. Dodson changed his mind when he saw Jack's fossils and how carefully Jack had interpreted that evidence. "Jack had made one of the great discoveries in dinosaur science."

Now we knew that at least one kind of dinosaur was a caring parent. It had fed and protected its helpless young in huge nesting colonies. Jack's discovery provided a new vision of how some dinosaurs behaved—much like birds today. Jack's evidence also suggested new conclusions about how dinosaurs grew.

Dinosaurs were long thought of as cold-blooded, without the high energy of warm-blooded animals like mammals and birds. But it would take a cold-blooded crocodile a year to double its size as the baby duckbills did while in the nest. No modern animal we know of stays in the nest a whole year. Warm-blooded baby birds can double their size in a month or two. Maybe dinosaurs were more like warm-blooded birds than cold-blooded reptiles?

The *Maiasaura* colony was not the only treasure Jack uncovered at Egg Mountain and nearby Egg Island. Jack's team also found eggs and nests of much smaller dinosaurs. In one nest Jack's group found nineteen eggs. What kind of dinosaur had laid them?

Back in the laboratory, Jack used an X-ray machine to look into these eggs. There were bones still inside. Carefully, he cut open the eggs and chipped away the sediment. Jack found the tiny bones of a

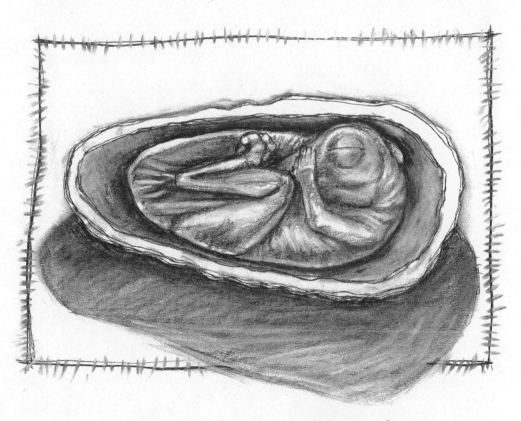

Orodromeus embryo in egg, artist's restoration

hypsilophodontid, a slim plant-eater that ran on its hind legs. With tiny picks and a microscope that magnified the image of the bones one hundred times, it took Jack most of four winters to remove the tiny skeleton from the egg.

This was a new kind of hypsilophodontid, less than ten feet in length when fully grown, including its long tail. Jack (and his colleague Dave Weishampel) called the swift little dinosaur *Orodromeus,* "the mountain runner." Its species name was *makelai,* in honor of Bob Makela. *Orodromeus* was the first dinosaur ever named from an embryo.

Fossils of newly hatched *Orodromeus* showed that the baby mountain runner had hardened bone tips, unlike the baby maiasaurs. These dinosaurs were born "up and running." They didn't need care from their parents to survive. So in the same time and place, two different kinds of dinosaurs had led very different kinds of lives. The big species of plant-eaters were raising their babies in the nest, while the smaller ones had much more independent young.

Everywhere Jack looked around Egg Mountain—and some places he didn't look—he found dinosaurs. Take the time Jack tried to stake up his tent.

Jack and most of his crew sleep in tepees now. Tepees are cooler than tents in the hot sun and more stable in the eighty-mile-an-hour winds that sweep across the plains. Since they have a smokehole at the peak, you can cook inside tepees. They look pretty, too.

Back when Jack was digging at Egg Mountain, he had a tent. When he tried to hammer his tent peg into the ground to make a camp, he struck a rock. He moved his tent and tried again. Another rock. Everywhere Jack tried to put the tent, he struck rocks. He dug around a bit and found that instead of rocks, he was running up against the bones of duckbilled dinosaurs. Instead of a campground, Jack had a new quarry. This one was a bonebed of thousands of duckbilled dinosaurs, killed in some disaster. Here was proof duckbilled dinosaurs traveled in, and sometimes died in, huge herds.

More than ten years after Jack found it, the "Camptosaur" Quarry (a joke name for the dinosaur site, which came from "camp") is still a source of bones for diggers. Though Jack and his crew have moved on to other digs, kids and their parents come to Egg Mountain every summer from around the world to stay in tepees for a week and dig up the "Camptosaur" bones.

Egg Mountain has become one of the greatest success stories in all of paleontology. In six years of digging, Jack and his teams scraped and shoveled away more than ten tons of Egg Mountain rock to find fossils of mammals, lizards, insects, and plants.

At Egg Mountain, Jack had found the first embryo of a dinosaur. He had named two kinds of dinosaurs. He had found skeletons of duckbilled and hypsilophodontid dinosaurs, from embryos to full-grown animals. And although no one had ever found dinosaur eggs or nests in North America before, Jack and his team of volunteers had found dozens of eggs from three kinds of dinosaurs.

The third kind of egg belonged to a small and little-known meat-eating dinosaur. It was named *Troodon,* "wound tooth." Teeth of *Troodon* were mixed in with some of the hypsilophodontid skeletons, so Jack thought maybe the mysterious *Troodon* was a hypsilophodontid, the first one to eat meat.

Jack Horner had found so many fossils at Egg Mountain because he knew where and how to look for them. But luck is always important in paleontology. As the rest of the *Troodon* story shows, Jack has been lucky as well as talented at finding dinosaurs.

Troodon had been known for nearly a century, but only from a few teeth. Just what the dinosaur looked like was very much a mystery, even after Jack found its teeth and eggs at Egg Mountain.

Then, one spring afternoon in 1983, Jack Horner took a drive north to Alberta, Canada, to visit a friend, dinosaur scientist Phil Currie. Dr. Currie was out in the fossil-rich badlands himself. He was supervising the building of a new fossil museum, the Royal Tyrrell Museum of Palaeontology.

Phil and Jack decided to take a walk. As good dinosaur scientists do, they walked with their heads down, always on the lookout for fossils.

Soon Jack found the jaw of a small dinosaur sticking out of a rocky hillside. He knew it was a meat-eater by its sharp teeth.

Phil Currie, an expert on meat-eaters' teeth, could tell even more. He recognized the teeth of as those of *Troodon.* He knew Jack had found the first *Troodon* jaw ever discovered!

Phil decided he would return the next day with his crew to excavate the fossil. But it rained hard the next day. And it kept raining for a week afterward. By the time Dr. Currie could return to the site, mud had washed over the fossil. Though he looked for hours, Dr. Currie couldn't find the jaw. At last, he gave up his search.

Two years later, Dr. Horner came back to Alberta to visit Dr. Currie. Again they took a walk near the museum. And again, Dr. Horner looked down and saw the *Troodon* jawbone.

To have found the same small bone in the vast badlands was a discovery as rare as finding a needle in a haystack—twice. This time, Dr. Currie put a bright-orange flag in the ground by the fossil until he and his crew could remove it carefully from the rock.

The beautiful jaw and its teeth were brought to the museum. Under Dr. Currie's careful study, Jack learned much about *Troodon* and its teeth. Here was not a little hypsilophodontid but a human-sized dinosaur with nimble fingers, big eyes, and the largest brain of any animal of its time.

That discovery led to many other *Troodon* finds. In Montana, Dr. Horner and his team found skeletons from a group of *Troodon* that appear to have died in a drought. Perhaps these intelligent dinosaurs had traveled together and hunted in packs, as wolves do today.

Jack would make many more finds in Montana in 1980s, with more time for dinosaur hunting. In the late 1970s Princeton decided to close its paleontology department and gave its fossils to Yale University. Jack went looking for another job. He found one with the Academy of Natural Sciences in Philadelphia, where he stayed for a few years, working in Philadelphia during the winters and making great discoveries at Egg Mountain in the summer.

Those discoveries made Jack famous as the man who found baby dinosaurs. Montanans were especially proud of Jack's discoveries. In 1982, Montana State University in Bozeman offered Jack the job of assistant curator at its Museum of the Rockies. In the winter he would teach classes, organize the museum's fossil collections, write scientific papers, and clean fossils. In the summer he'd be off investigating new fossil sites in Montana. Jack jumped at the chance.

CHAPTER 5

The Treasures of Landslide Butte

Remember the drawer full of eggshells at the Smithsonian? Well, back in Montana in 1984, Jack finally had time to get to the site where Charles Gilmore had found those eggshells more than fifty years earlier. Landslide Butte stood over a hundred miles north of Egg Mountain. It was a hilly patch of badlands on the Blackfoot Indian Reservation.

Though Gilmore had found eggshells at Landslide Butte, he apparently hadn't looked very closely at what else the place had to offer in the way of fossils. Jack did look, and what he saw astounded him. Over a few square miles of hills and gullies, Jack found two huge bonebeds of droop-horned dinosaurs called *Styracosaurus*—spiked lizard, relatives of *Triceratops*. And he found three bonebeds full of duckbilled dinosaurs, some with crests and others without crests. As Jack recalls in *Digging Dinosaurs*, "there were hillsides with bones just jumping out of them."

The most amazing find of all at Landslide Butte was a duckbill nesting ground of staggering size—a mile wide and three miles long. There were three layers of nests, one on top of the other across this enormous breeding ground. Where Jack had to crawl and poke in the dirt to find eggshells at Egg Mountain, at Landslide Butte he could

gather eggshells by the shovelful. And bones of duckbills were *everywhere,* from what Jack figured to have been a huge herd killed in some disaster, like a drought.

Jack estimated there were 53 *million* dinosaur fossils at Landslide Butte. Many were broken into small pieces. But some fossils were so enormous that even Bob Makela's clever homemade sleds couldn't haul them off the hillsides. Two styracosaur skulls, each weighing more than a ton, had to be strapped up and airlifted by huge Army helicopters.

Jack and his crew worked several summers at Landslide Butte collecting dinosaur treasures. A crew worked six days straight, then drove off to town for showers and a day off. One day Bob Makela went off to town for supplies. He never came back. Word came to Jack at Landslide Butte that Bob had been killed in a car wreck.

Jack mourned his best friend quietly and, in his own quiet way, took over the job of managing camp. And in 1986, when Jack's discoveries won him a surprise "genius grant" of $200,000 from the MacArthur Foundation, he didn't show many feelings, either. Mick Hager, his former boss at the Museum of the Rockies, remembers, "When I called Jack to tell him he'd won the prize, all he said was 'Gee, I've got to walk around and think about this.'"

Fame and success didn't change Jack. The foundation's gift did allow him to move into his own home for the first time. Jack was divorced by then, and he's been married and divorced a second time. His long summers away in the field made it hard to keep up a marriage.

CHAPTER 6

Fame and *T. rex*

Nowadays, as the world's best-known dinosaur scientist, Jack is liable to be called off to far-flung places any time of the year. He leads expeditions to Mongolia and Mexico. He gives talks in museums from New York (at the American Museum, where he once studied) to New Zealand. With Britain's Princess Diana, he opened a dinosaur exhibit in London, and with a Japanese movie star, Jack opened an amusement park of robot dinosaurs.

In the winter of 1992, Jack spent several days on the set of the movie *Jurassic Park*, advising director Steven Spielberg and his crew on how to make the dinosaurs look, move, and sound in a realistic way. Jack didn't agree with everything the moviemakers did, but he wasn't picky. "Geez, it's only a movie!" he said. "They are the best dinosaurs any people ever made."

In Bozeman, Jack's daily life has remained much the same to this day, though he is now chief curator of paleontology and head of a large department. He works through the long, cold winters, slowly typing papers in his windowless basement office and examining fossils in the laboratory and collection rooms nearby.

Each day Jack takes time to feed and pet the monitor lizards, snakes, and green iguana that he keeps in his office. The alligators, caiman, and python raised in his lab have grown so big they are now kept at a local fish hatchery. Since he likes to bowl, Jack has fashioned a homemade bowling alley on a long corridor in the museum basement.

He works surrounded by his friends and longtime helpers, among them Carrie Ancell, his chief preparator, and his crew chief, Pat Leiggi. In the summer of 1988, Jack came across Bob Harmon, a gun-toting fossil hunter, walking the badlands where Jack was digging dinosaurs. Instead of shooing him away, Jack hired him.

Though Jack never completed the work for a degree, he now has graduate students of his own. They come to *him* to get their degrees in paleontology.

What Jack, his students, and his crew work on each winter still has mostly to do with the fossils they and Jack find the summer before. And every summer, Jack keeps turning up more amazing dinosaurs.

Though he still likes nothing better than finding a duckbilled dinosaur, it isn't always duckbills that Jack digs up. He found the first herd of *Triceratops* ever uncovered. He unearthed what may be the first known eggs from a flying reptile, a pterosaur. And he found a

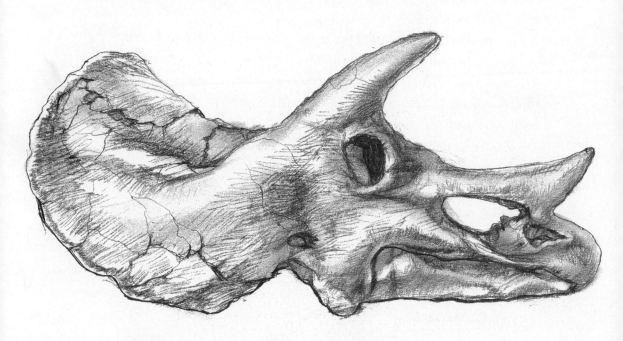

Triceratops head

Pterosaurs—flying reptiles

giant browsing dinosaur on the ranch of television-network owner Ted Turner and his wife, actress Jane Fonda.

Now that Jack is so well known, sometimes other people bring *him* dinosaurs. In 1988, a rancher named Kathy Wankel showed Jack two bones she had found while hiking. Mrs. Wankel brought those bones three hundred miles from western Montana because she thought they might be special.

Jack took one look at the bones and knew Kathy Wankel was right. Jack had never seen bones like them, but from their size and shape he knew they could be only one thing—the arm bones of a *Tyrannosaurus rex*. That enormous meat-eater may be the best known of all dinosaurs. But in a hundred years of knowing *T. rex*, scientists have found only about a dozen good skeletons. Before Kathy Wankel, no one had ever found *T. rex*'s arms.

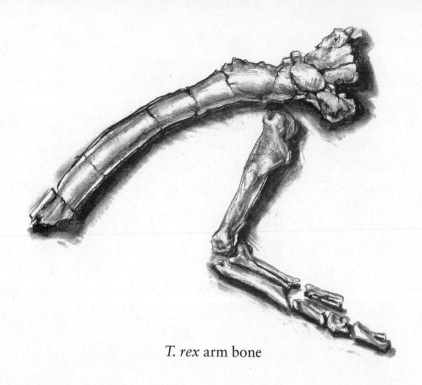

T. rex arm bone

Jack sent his crew out to investigate. Pat and the others discovered much more of the dinosaur beneath the surface. In the summer of 1990, Jack led his crew out to the hill where Kathy Wankel had made her discovery. In less than a month, they dug away more than fifty tons of sandstone and uncovered the most complete *T. rex* yet known, nearly an entire skeleton. Almost forty feet long, it had teeth the size of bananas and might have weighed seven tons in life.

Parts of the skeleton, still surrounded by rock, needed to be exposed and wrapped in plaster for safe handling. It was heavy, but delicate, work. In the ancient stream channel where the dinosaur had died, the skull had broken away and slid next to the animal's hips. On his hands and knees, Jack carefully tunneled a separation between the skull of *T. rex* and the hip bones. That way, both groups of bones could be safely plastered and removed.

A front-end loader and a flatbed truck were brought in to the badlands to move the heavy blocks containing *T. rex*'s bones. *T. rex* was lugged in big white-jacketed pieces back to Jack's lab in the basement of the Museum of the Rockies. But some of the blocks were so heavy, they would have fallen right through the floor. So Jack's crew had to begin cleaning them off on the loading dock.

It took nearly three years to finish the job of cleaning *T. rex*. But the job of studying *T. rex* is still going on. Jack says, "I'm no expert on *T. rex*," but he has come up with some interesting theories about it. "People think of *T. rex* as a vicious predator," says Jack. "But I think it spent most of its time eating things already dead."

Jack and his team have made some surprising discoveries from Kathy Wankel's *T. rex*. The little arms of *T. rex* were only as long as our own but ten times more powerful! What *T. rex* used those arms for remains a mystery. "They couldn't even touch each other, or reach its mouth," says Jack. "I don't think those arms were good for much."

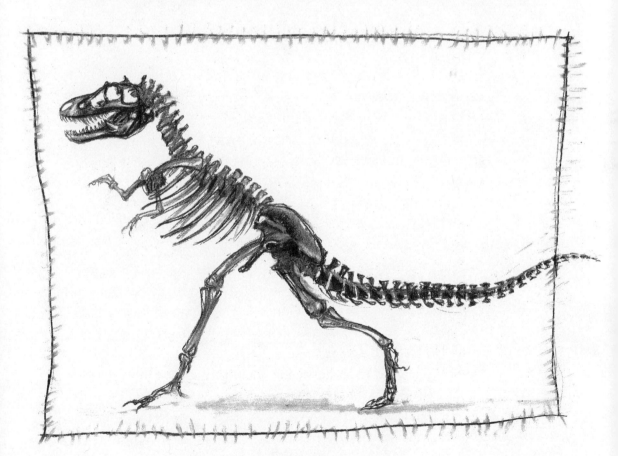

Most complete *T. rex* skeleton

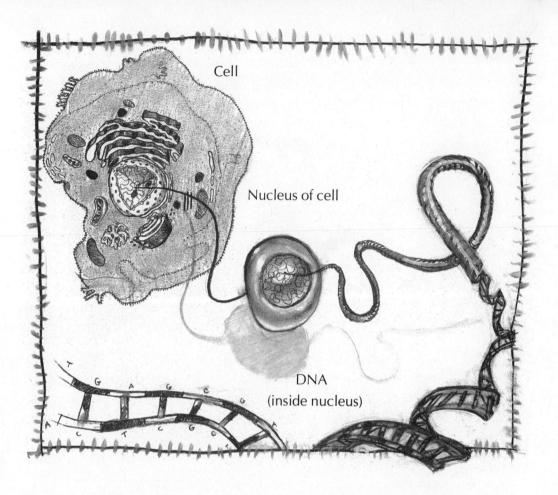

Cell

Nucleus of cell

DNA
(inside nucleus)

A student of Jack's may have found something very tiny and special inside the hug leg bone of the *T. rex*. It appears under the microscope to be a blood cell. Inside this cell is what appears to be the DNA of the *T. rex*. If so, it is the first dinosaur DNA ever found.

DNA is the complex string of molecules that contains the genetic code for making any particular living thing. We don't know how to bring any animal to life from its DNA. That happens only in movies like *Jurassic Park*. "I wouldn't want to bring back a *T. rex* if I could," says Jack. "They're really scary."

But even a bit of *T. rex* DNA would help Jack and other scientists understand much about what ancestors dinosaurs came from, how dinosaurs were related to each other, and what makes dinosaurs different from all other animals.

CHAPTER 7

A Day in a Duckbill's Life

Jack and his team are busy at work in the laboratory, looking closely at the bone cells of dinosaurs and other animals. Now that Jack has discovered so many dinosaurs at each phase of their lives—embryo to adult—he can begin to answer some questions about how fast they grew.

The bones of baby duckbilled dinosaurs are full of holes, like the bones of birds. The holes are spaces for blood vessels. Lots of blood flowed through those bones, helping the babies to grow fast. How fast? Jack now has some precise answers.

Jack figures, "Baby duckbills hatched out of their eggs at about eighteen inches long. They grew to three and half feet in about three and a half weeks. They reached nine feet the first year. They got to be adult size, about twenty feet long, in about four and a half years." That's the fast growth rate of a warm-blooded animal.

In the laboratory, Jack has learned much about how duckbilled dinosaurs grew. Out in the badlands, he's discovered how they lived, even how different ones developed. The answers have come to Jack while he walks along the borders of the ancient seaway that flowed millions of years ago across what is now Montana.

Before Jack Horner found dinosaur eggs in Montana, no one knew where to look for them. The answer, Jack discovered, was not *by* the ancient sea. Instead he looked *between* the ancient sea and the mountains, on what was once the upper coastal plain. Dinosaurs seem to have moved inland, away from the coast, to lay their eggs.

Jack also learned that if you followed the changing course of the sea over millions of years, you could discover a lot about which dinosaurs lived where and when.

The duckbilled dinosaurs Jack Horner finds come mostly from the Two Medicine Formation, a layer of rock in western Montana that is two thousand feet thick. Over millions of years, sand and mud had washed in from the great inland sea and down from the mountains to build these rocks. Sometimes the sea was wide and pushed up close to the mountains. Other times the sea pulled back and left broad deltas far from the mountains.

Different duckbilled dinosaurs developed in these different habitats. The fancy-crested dinosaurs, the lambeosaurs, seem to have lived close to the shore and thrived when the sea was low. The duckbills without crests, like *Maiasaura*, lived in the uplands.

It's rare that we know any extinct animals well enough to say in such detail how they lived and developed over time. But Jack Horner knows duckbills that well. After years of collecting dinosaurs, Jack can re-create the changing world of duckbilled dinosaurs in Montana over millions of years. But he can also imagine, as no one has before, just what the daily lives of duckbills were like.

Picture a green valley between the sea and the mountains. A huge herd of duckbilled dinosaurs is striding on long hind legs, heading south to feed in the forests during the mild winter. They've come from several hundred miles north. There they spent the spring, hatching their fast-growing babies, and the summer, feeding on lush plants in the long northern summer light.

Their heads bob as they slowly march. Adults guard the front and sides of the herd, with the half-grown young in the center. The grown-ups blow toots from their huge crests to keep the group together or to warn of an approaching meat-eater.

The marching duckbills pass groups of squat, armored dinosaurs feeding, and large herds of big-horned dinosaurs. Speedy hypsilophodonts race by, and in the twilight, packs of *Troodon* hunt small mammals. In forest glades, the duckbills pause to feed, working their jaws up and down, in and out, to grind great wads of plants.

We'll never know exactly how dinosaurs looked, nor every detail about how they lived. But we know that some such scenes happened 75 million years ago, because of the fossils Jack Horner has discovered and interpreted.

When Jack is out walking in the badlands, it's not hard for him to imagine the world as it was when duckbills lived. But he'd rather track down further clues these dinosaurs left behind, so he can learn still more of their story. Jack hopes most of all for more days like his birthday, a few Junes ago. Jack was up and about early in the morning, walking in the badlands, looking for fossils along the Two Medicine River. Suddenly, he came upon the flank of a hill that shimmered in the morning light. The hillside was glowing with the reflection of thousands of dinosaur bones.

"Jack's Birthday Site," as the hill became known, produced the fossils of hundreds of duckbills and other dinosaurs. It was the best birthday present Jack ever had.

For, as Jack Horner likes to say, "Duckbill dinosaurs are neat animals. *Really* neat."

INDEX/GLOSSARY

FURTHER READING

SOURCE

For information on digs, museum exhibits, and scientifically recommended children's publications, contact the nonprofit Dinosaur Society, 200 Carleton Avenue, East Islip, NY 11730. The society publishes the monthly *Dino Times* for children and the quarterly *Dinosaur Report* for adults.

BOOKS

The Complete T. rex by John R. Horner and Don Lessem
(New York: Simon & Schuster, 1993). A heavily illustrated book for older readers on all that is known and speculated about the king of the dinosaurs.

Digging Dinosaurs by John R. Horner and James Gorman
(New York: Workman, 1989). A slim illustrated book for older readers detailing Jack Horner's discoveries.

Digging Up Tyrannosaurus rex by John R. Horner and Don Lessem
(New York: Crown, 1993). An illustrated children's book detailing the excavation of the largest *T. rex* yet known.

The Dinosaur Society Dinosaur Encyclopedia by Don Lessem and Donald F. Glut.
(New York: Random House, 1993). The most current, thorough dictionary of dinosaurs, well illustrated.

The Illustrated Encyclopedia of Dinosaurs by David Norman.
(Avenal, NJ: Crescent, 1985). The best and best-illustrated reference on all aspects of dinosaur behavior and evolution for older readers.

Maia, A Dinosaur Grows Up by John R. Horner and James Gorman.
(Philadelphia: Running Press, 1986). A beautifully illustrated children's story based on Dr. Horner's pioneering research.